POETRY

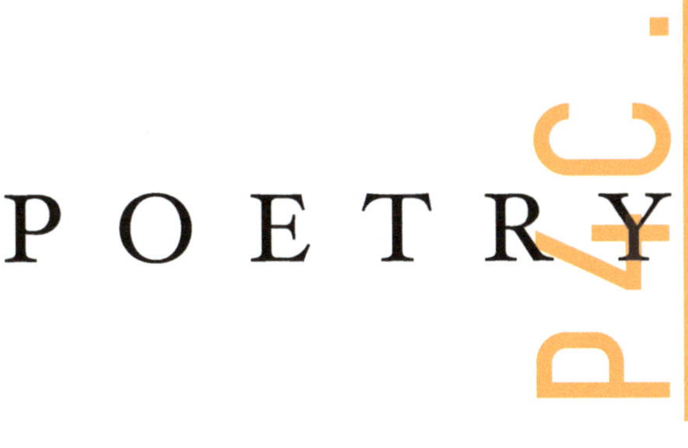

for

CORPORATIONS

Bruna MORI

with KYLIE KING and WENDY BELT

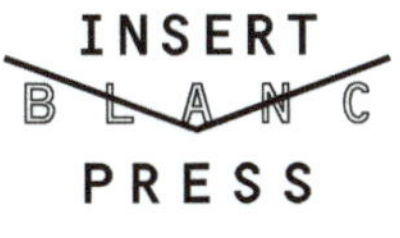

Los Angeles

Poetry for Corporations | ISBN:978-1-947322-94-3 | Insert Blanc Press | ©2019

Poetry for Corporations is a selection of my copy written for notable brands between 2000 - 2015, repurposed and arranged in sections on content, form, and correspondence. Stock photography curated by writer Kylie King; design by creative director Wendy Belt. Conceptual, confessional, or constraint-based, there is a place for parroting one's livelihood, to remember when humans were encouraged to write like machines, as machines are now asked to have humanity.

Poetry for Corporations marks a vanishing era. Raw copy deck formats document a moment before AI transitions a livelihood--a time when we became ghosts for corporations, cobbling together taxonomies, disclaimers, word counts based on calculated attention spans, top 10 benign adjectives in some combination that conveyed the essence of a brand.

Most poetry about corporations looks at the phenomena through the lens of disaster capitalism (or more recently, accelerationism). *Poetry for Corporations* is the lightly placed disaster (or potential) itself.

- BRUNA MORI

TABLE *of* CONTENTS

CAMERA
AD

A airport, travel, phone, business, smartphone, passenger, plane, asian, mobile, people, cell, girl, happy, waiting, suitcase, text, air, professional, lady, cellphone, smart, sms, gate, terminal, international, flight, baggage, boarding, female, young, businesswoman, lifestyle, adult, beautiful, businessperson, carry-on, caucasian, departure, internet, journey, message, mixed, person, portrait, race, sitting, smiling, texting, transport, traveler, women : 178265705

Compact cutie.

Blink proof.
Fits your purse.

Sleek, stylish
and mobile like you.

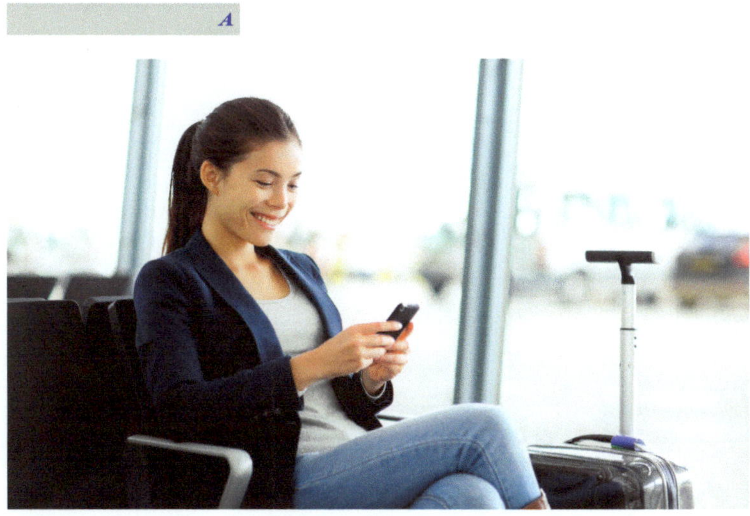

HANNAH,
HANNAH,
HANNAH

B Education and technology - group of students taking selfie with tablet pc at school. // people, selfie, school, group, young, high, team, laughing, education, happy, tablet, technology, college, classroom, friends, funny, international, african, american, app, application, attractive, boys, class, classmates, communication, e-learning, faces, fun, girls, guys, having, men, modern, multiethnic, networking, pc, portrait, self, smiling, social, students, studying, taking, teamwork, teenagers, teens, together, university, women : 256173130

C Technology concept - group of students taking selfie with tablet pc. // picture, social, people, technology, video, group, self, photo, school, making, college, portrait, classroom, talking, team, class, selfie, fun, african, break, handsome, teenagers, university, high, young, american, attractive, boys, campus, chatting, classmates, communicating, communication, education, friendly, friends, girls, happy, having, international, laughing, men, networking, new, smiling, students, studying, taking, teens, women : 148728104

Step inside it.

Coming this fall,
's new DVD:
"Life's What You Make It".

High school classes.
with lessons in love.
It's double trouble for !

You've got a backstage pass
to the lives of .

B

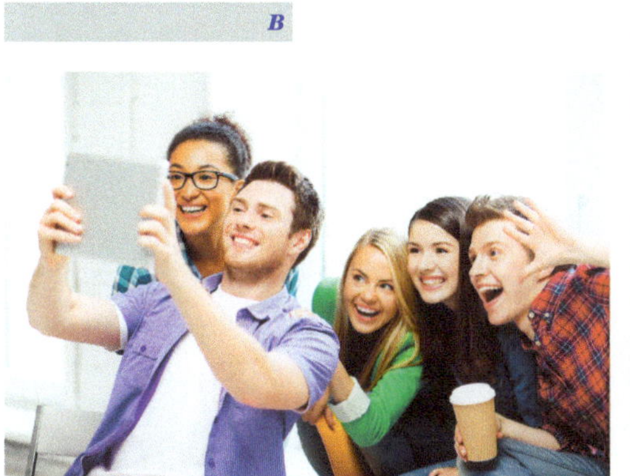

C

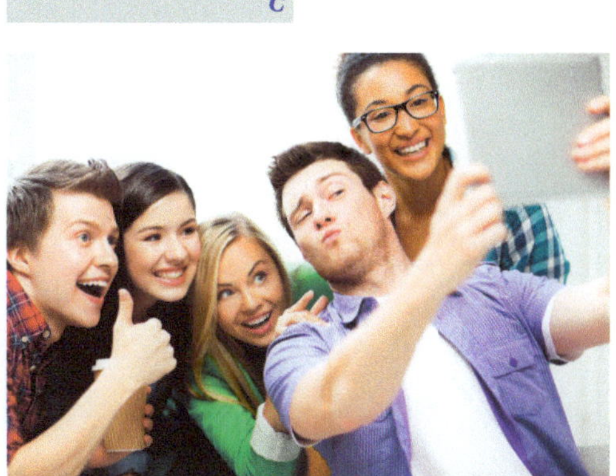

CALL *to* ACTION

D Successful young professional man celebrates success holding new contract documents. Entrepreneur enjoys success in job. // african, america, professional, job, promotion, happy, businessman, money, black, student, worker, proud, man, male, lawyer, guy, deal, corporate, contract, business, successful, latin, achievement, building, celebrating, celebration, cheerful, city, copyspace, documents, employee, entrepreneur, ethnic, expression, face, gesturing, glad, goal, handsome, happiness, modern, outdoors, outside, papers, people, person, success, suit, urban, winner : 280333736

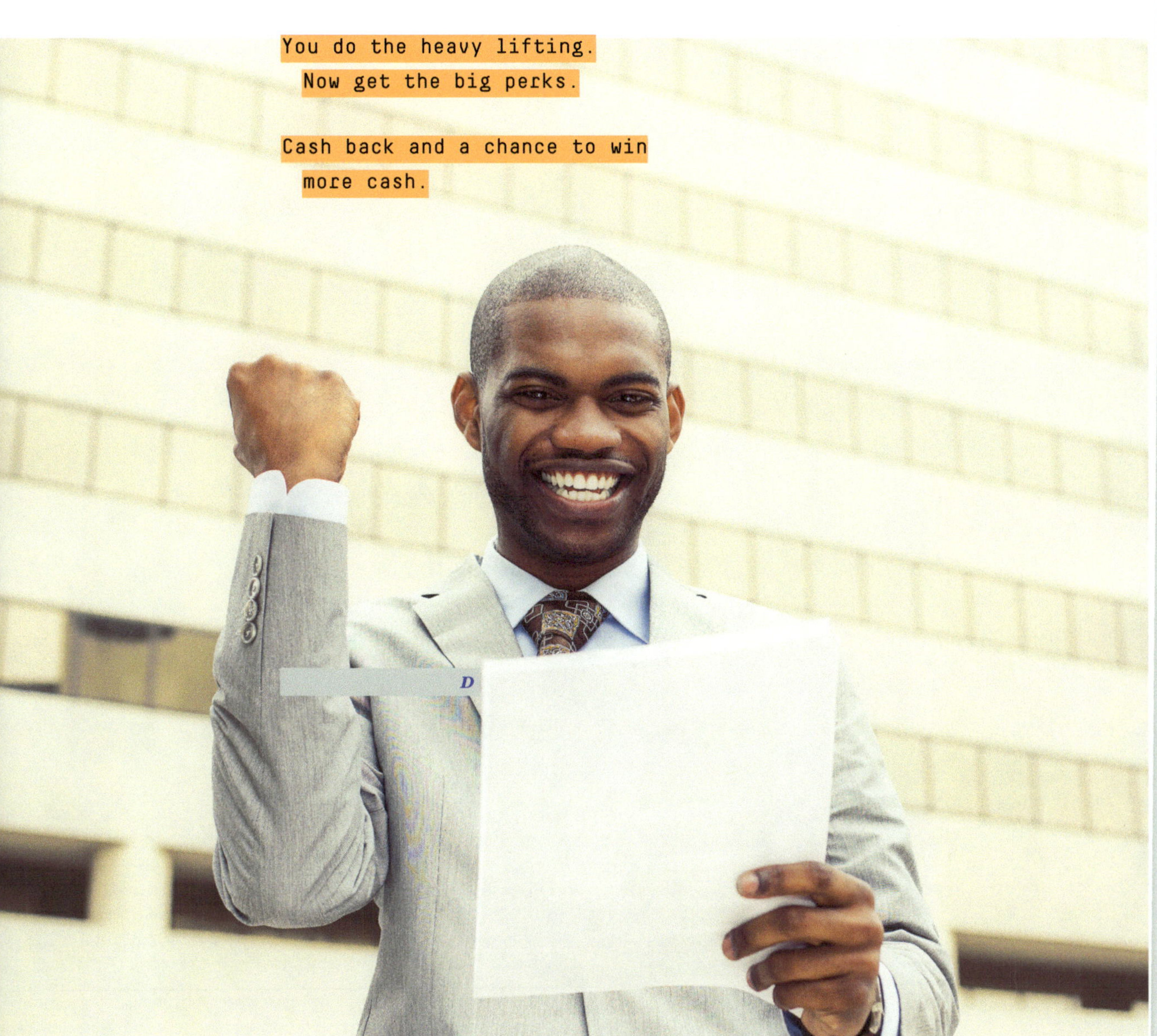
You do the heavy lifting.
Now get the big perks.
Cash back and a chance to win
more cash.

PROMO INSERT

E

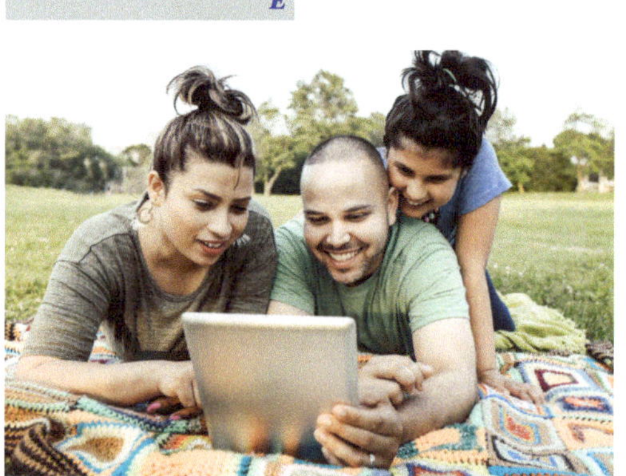

E Video blog for family. // picnic, 30-4 years, 35-9 years, 8-9 years, adult, black hair, bonding, canada, care, cheerful, child, childhood, daughter, embracing, emigration and immigration, emoticon, enjoyment, family, family with one child, father, females, fun, girls, happiness, healthy eating, healthy lifestyle, horizontal, immigrant, internet, latin american and hispanic ethnicity, lifestyles, looking at camera : 697770126

[HEADER - Panel 2]

It's extra-easy!

[HEADER - Panel 3]

It's extra-exciting!

[INSIDE]

[HEADER]

The [illegible] Extras One Million Sweepstakes
You could win 1,000,000 dollars.

Why wait to start enjoying increased customer activity and loyalty? You can start developing your program right now. Just visit [illegible] Online [link to: http://www.us.[illegible]online.com] or contact your [illegible] Account Executive for more information.

[illegible]'s Zero Liability Policy covers U.S.-issued cards only and does not apply to commercial credit cards, ATM transactions, or PIN transactions not processed by [illegible]. Cardholder must notify card issuer promptly of any unauthorized use. Consult issuer for additional details or visit [illegible].com/security.

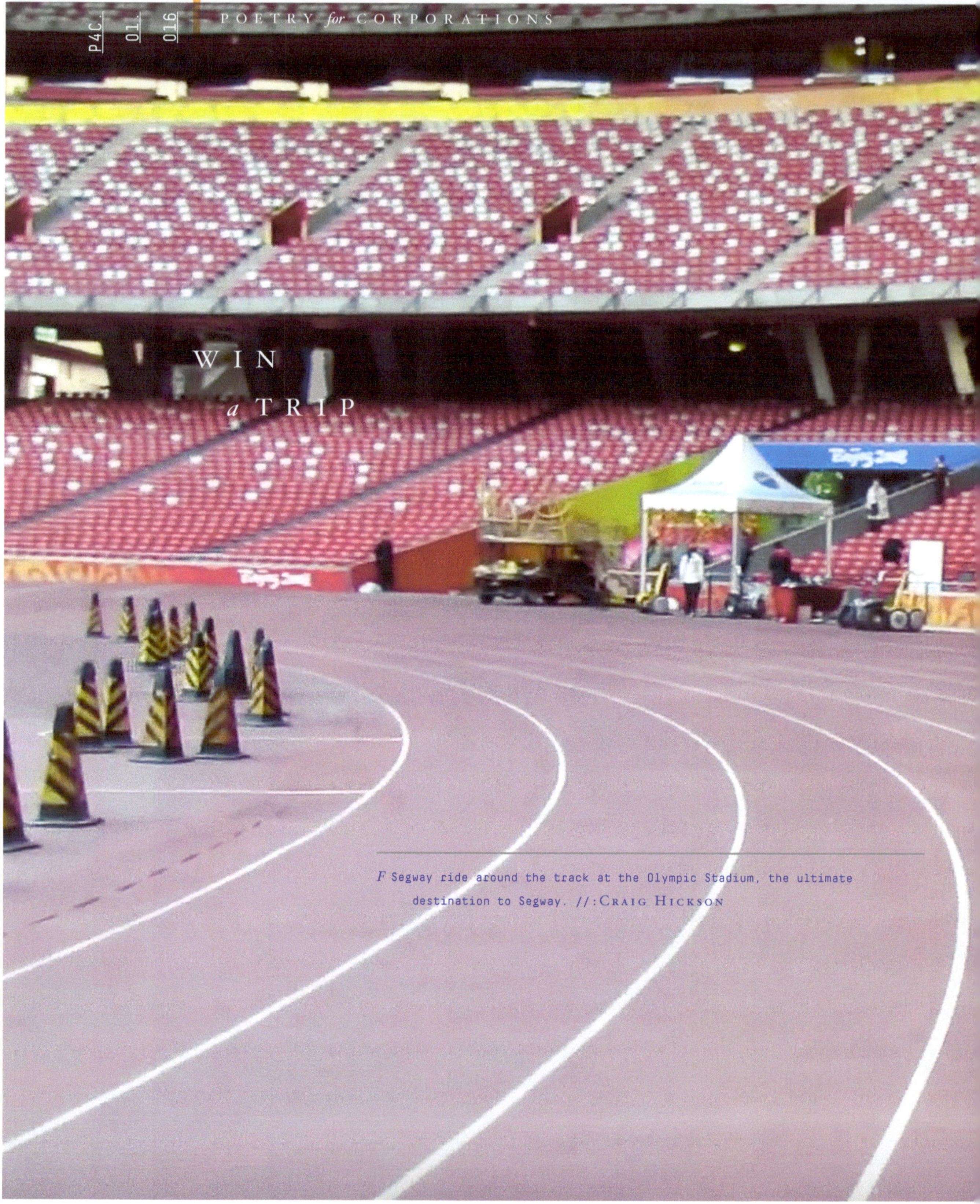

WIN *a* TRIP

F Segway ride around the track at the Olympic Stadium, the ultimate destination to Segway. //:Craig Hickson

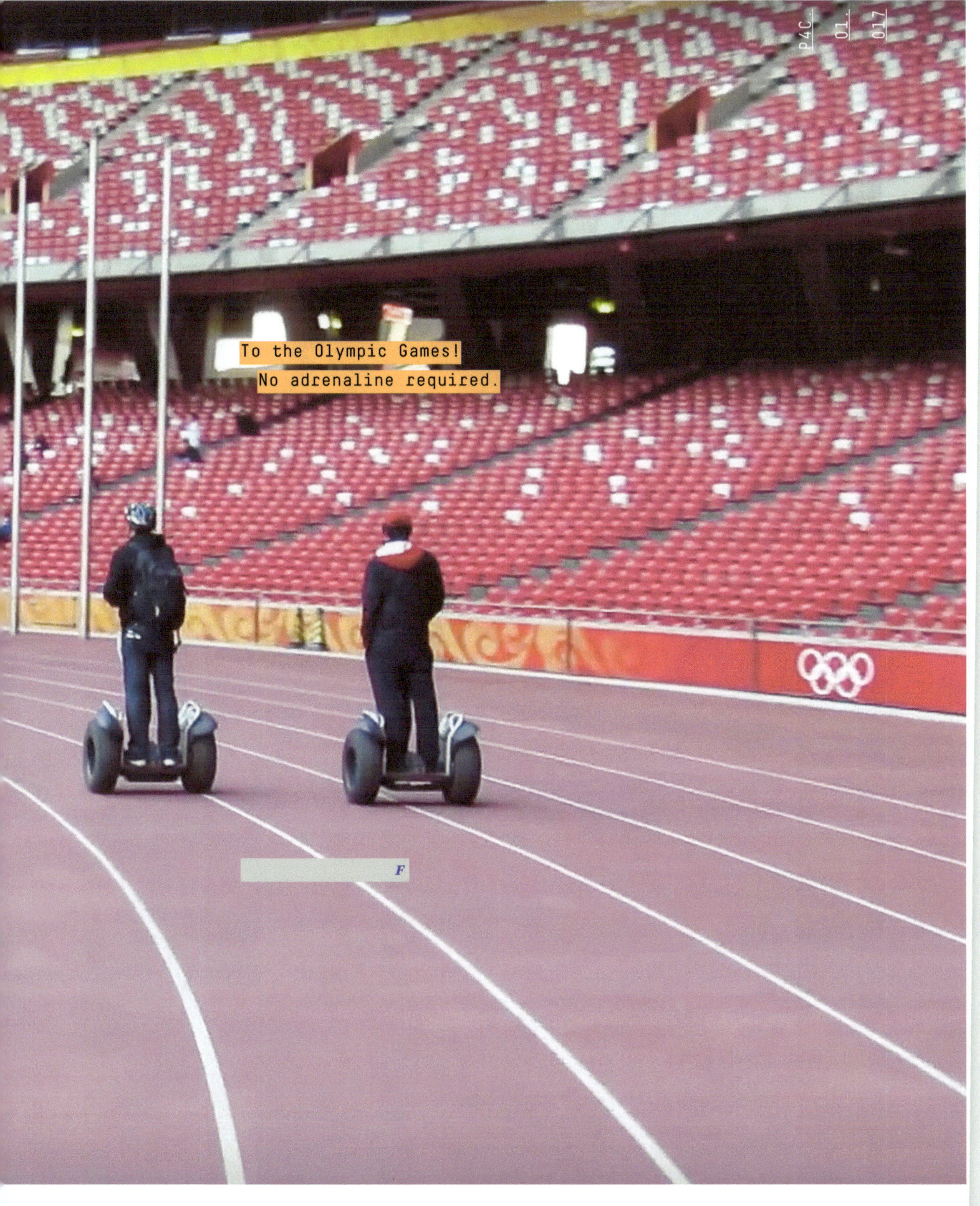

To the Olympic Games!
No adrenaline required.

WISH WE
WERE HERE,
[REGISTERED
USER]

[SUBJECT]

[REGISTERED USER] wants you to accompany them to the Olympic Games!

[FIELDS]

To: [REFERRED USER NAME]
To: [REFERRED USER EMAIL ADDRESS]
From: [REGISTERED USER NAME]
From: [REGISTERED USER EMAIL ADDRESS]

[IMAGE OF STADIUM]

Wish we were here!

[GREETING]

Hi [REFERRED USER NAME],

[BODY]

Wouldn't it be great to cheer on our favorite athletes at the Olympic Games? If you enter The Fastest Way to [illegible] Sweepstakes [LINK], we could be on our way to winning an action-packed vacation for two.

You can enter online [LINK] now. And when you use your [illegible] card from February 1 - April 30, you're automatically entered for a chance to win.

[CLOSING]

Your friend,
[REGISTERED USER NAME]

CROWD PLEASERS

G Woman preparing table. // adult, arranging, asian, at home, built structure, celebrations, conservatory, decoration, dining table, dinner, dinner party, dish, drinking glass, east asian ethnicity, en utensil, ethnicity, event, female, flower, food, glass, glasses, house, house interior, housing, image source, indoors, japanese ethnicity, kitsch, leaf, looking, meal, nature, one person, one young adult woman, only one woman, only women, only young women, party, place setting, plant, plant type, plate, preparation, preparing, smiling, structures, table, tableware, wine glass, woman, young, young adult, young woman : AWNNNJ

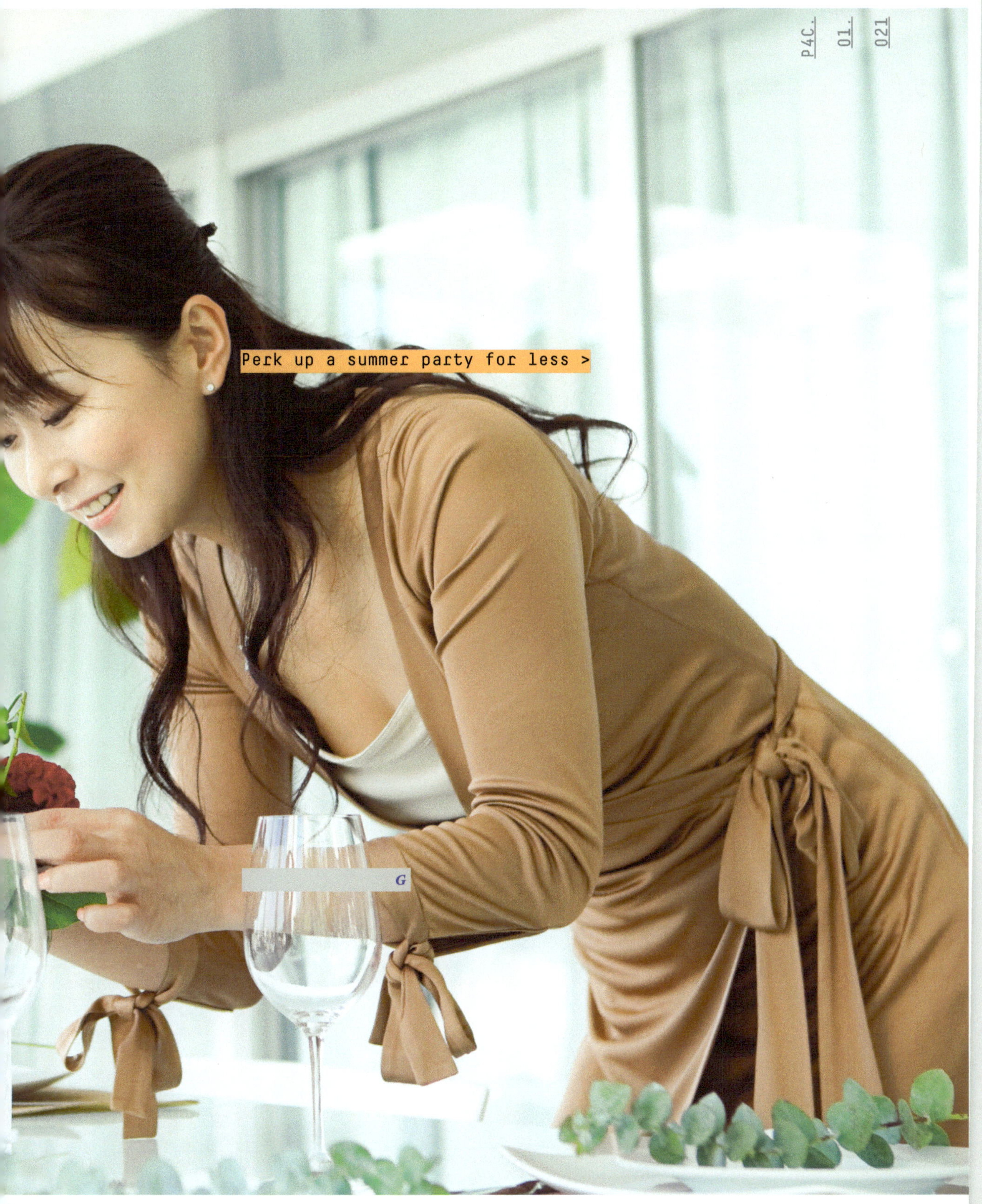
Perk up a summer party for less >
G

CONVENTION.
SWIM. STAY.

Convention. Swim. Stay.

Let's play.

Poolside recharge. Slipping and sliding.
Synchronized giggles. Full-body hydration.

Let's be real.

Blossoming palms. A rambling rose.
Confessing your love.
Claiming your pillow.

Let's just be better.

Rooms that inspire. Mattresses for jumping.
Coffee the way you love it. Where happy
just happens.

Let's Play. Let's be real.
Let's just be better.

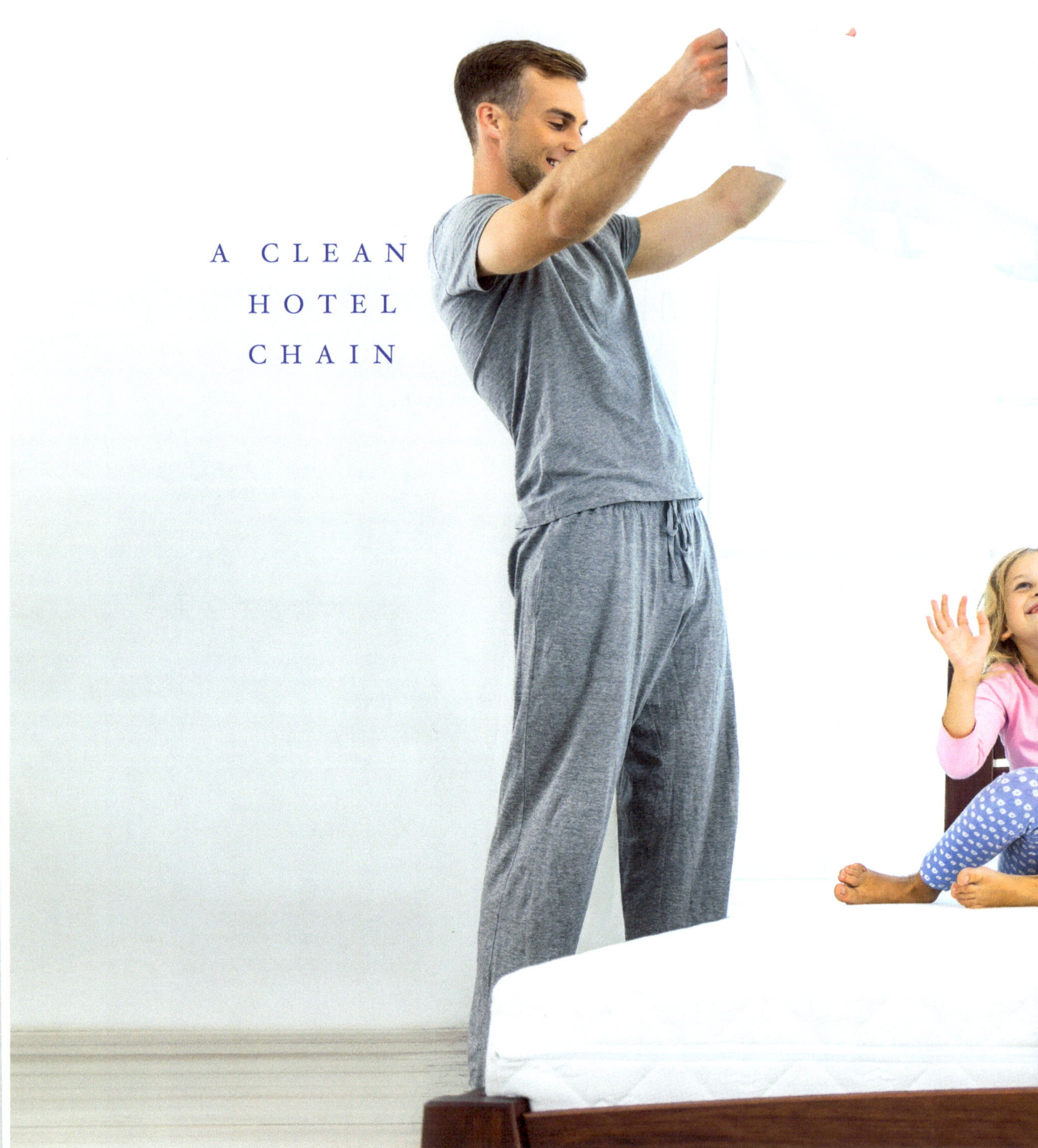

A CLEAN HOTEL CHAIN

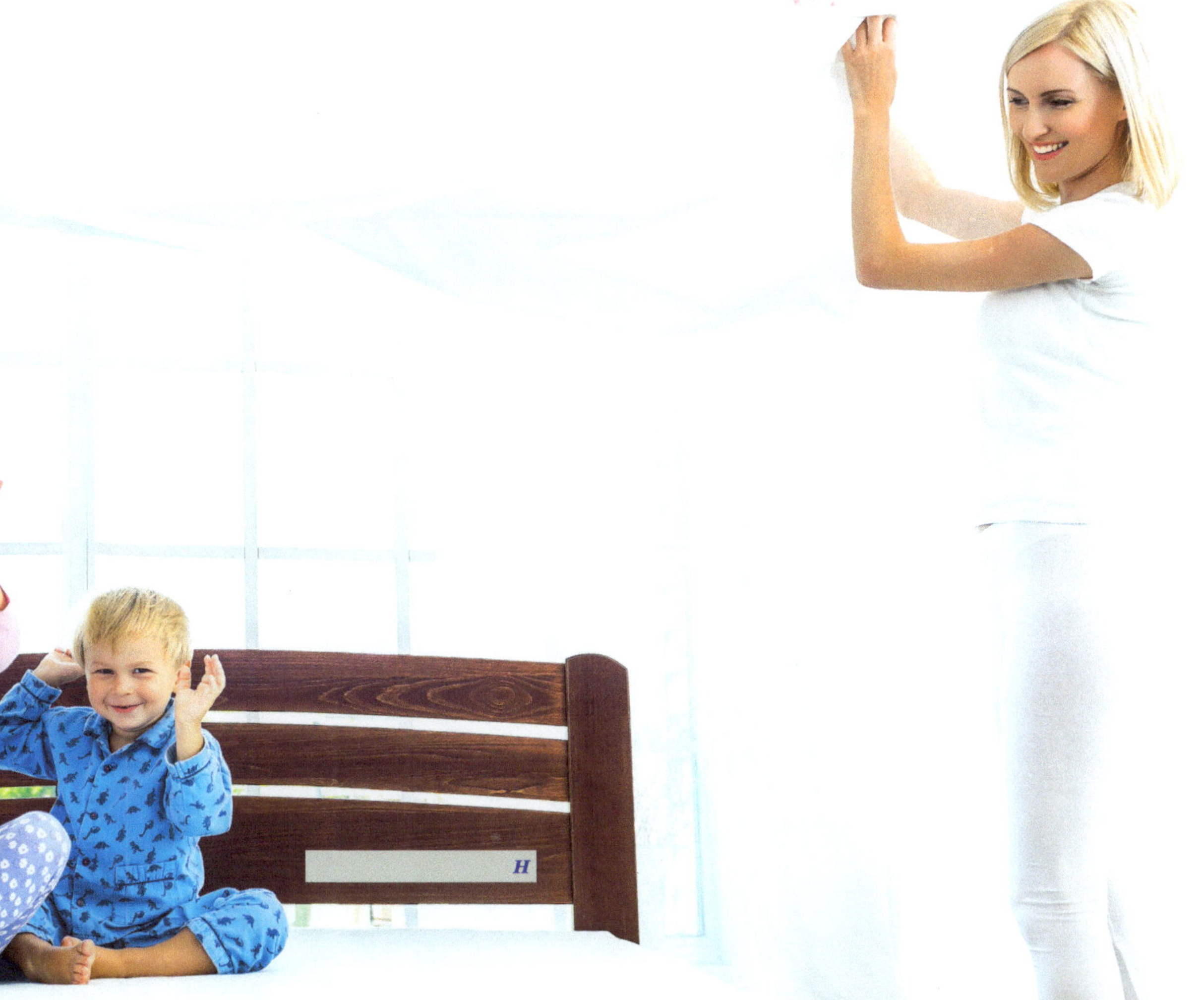

H Young nice family making bed. // mattress, child, bed - furniture, sleeping, two parents, caucasian, bedding, blanket, bedroom, clean, cozy, family, men, 2015, adult, backgrounds, beautiful people, beauty, comfortable, concepts, concepts & topics, covering design, domestic room, dreamlike, furniture, happiness, home interior, horizontal, hotel, indoors, lifestyles, love - emotion, luxury, luxury hotel, modern, offspring, people, photography, relaxation, softness, textile, togetherness, white color, women, young adult : 502288048

AT HOME *on the* ROAD

hotels are best
for working and unwinding.

You'll get free high-speed Internet
and a hearty Sunshine™ breakfast.

So kick back at the pool,
or relax on comfortable bedding.

And if you find a better price,
we'll match it.

META TAGS	
NEW PAGE TITLE	Online Hotel Booking and Travel Accommodations
NEW PAGE DESCRIPTION	offers quality hotel rooms at affordable rates. Reserve lodging for business or leisure travel online today.
CURRENT KEY WORDS	None
KEY WORDS TO ADD	clean, clean hotels, hotel brand, hotel deals, fast hotel booking, hotel travel, hotel reservations, hotel rooms, best hotels, hotel rates, hotel booking, book hotel reservations, vacation lodging, business lodging

[PROMO]

Reward Yourself!
With privileges, every day is
a summer holiday. Earn free hotel stays,
airline miles and more.
Join now >

BE PLEASANTLY SURPRISED

I

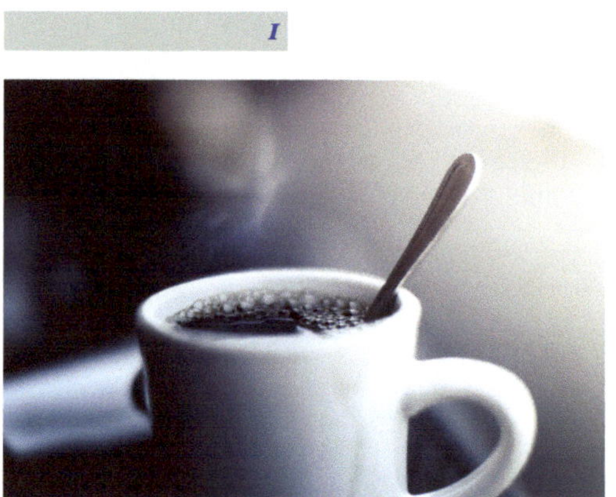

I Morning joe. //:Basheer Tome

Get a lot more for less—like more space
in your modern, well-furnished suite.

Start your business day with our free breakfast
and our friendly, responsive service.

Did we mention our free breakfast?

Get free Internet, and a microwave, too—
without paying a penny more.

META TAGS	
NEW PAGE TITLE	Business Lodging and Hotel Accommodations
NEW PAGE DESCRIPTION	offers over 500 quality hotels. Book a modern, well-furnished hotel suite with separate sleeping and sitting areas, plus free Internet.
CURRENT KEY WORDS	None
KEY WORDS TO ADD	cheap, cheap suites, cheap suites hotels, travel accommodations online, hotel booking, hotel reservations, hotel rooms, best hotels, hotel rates, hotel booking, book hotel reservations, business lodging

[PROMO]

Reward Yourself!
With privileges, every day is
a summer holiday. Earn free hotel stays,
airline miles and more.
Join now >

WE'VE GOT
LOCAL CHARM

Even our amenities are sensible.
Unwind on mattresses.
Connect with free high-speed Internet.
Pick up a paper with your morning coffee, and bacon.

META TAGS	
NEW PAGE TITLE	Discount Hotel Rates and Lodging
NEW PAGE DESCRIPTION	offers affordable hotel rooms with local charm. Make a hotel reservation at any of our 1,200 locally owned and operated locations.
CURRENT KEY WORDS	None
KEY WORDS TO ADD	affordable, affordable inn, affordable inn hotels, hotel deals, fast hotel booking, hotel reservations, hotel rooms, best hotels, hotel rates, hotel booking, book hotel reservations, vacation lodging

[PROMO]

Reward Yourself!
With privileges, every day is a summer holiday. Earn free hotel stays, airline miles and more.
Join now >

EXTEND YOUR
SATISFACTION
with EXTENDED
STAYS

You'll get more savings, the longer you stay.

Wake up each morning to a free continental breakfast—
or choose to cook for yourself in a fully equipped kitchen.

Guest laundry on site.
Weekly housekeeping.

All the comforts of home
at very attractive rates.

META TAGS	
NEW PAGE TITLE	Extended Stay Hotel and Online Reservations
NEW PAGE DESCRIPTION	Make an online reservation at [illegible] for an extended stay hotel room. You'll appreciate this inviting residential-style option.
CURRENT KEY WORDS	None
KEY WORDS TO ADD	extended stay hotel rates, extended stay hotel, hotel deals, fast hotel booking, hotel reservations, hotel rooms, best hotels, hotel rates, hotel booking, book hotel reservations, kicked out of house, business lodging

[PROMO]

Reward Yourself!
With [illegible] privileges, every day is
a summer holiday. Earn free hotel stays,
airline miles and more.
Join now >

ADVANCED SEARCH

[SIMPLE SEARCH]

Home

Search

By Destination

Along a Route

[FIELD]

Check-In

[FIELD]

Check-Out

[FIELD]

Rooms

[PULLDOWN]

Adults

[PULLDOWN]

Children

[ROLLOVER]

Kids under 18 stay for free, if they share the same room with their parents or grandparents and no additional bedding is required.

[PULLDOWN]

Special Rate

[PULLDOWN]

[BUTTON]

Find Hotels

[BUTTON]
Advanced Search

[ROLLOVER]
Expand your search for more customized results.

[ADVANCED SEARCH]
Tell us more:
Price Range
[SLIDER]
$0-$50
$50-$100
$100-$150
$150-$200
$200-$300
$300+

Preferences
[DROPDOWN]
Select Amenities
Pet-Friendly
Pool
Internet Access
Room Service
Business Area
Fitness Center
Restaurant

Search within

[DROPDOWN]

5mi/8km

10mi/16km

25mi/40km

50mi/80km

75mi/120km

Sort by

[DROPDOWN]

Rating

Price

Distance from destination

[CHECKBOX]

Only show hotels with rooms available.

[BUTTONS]

Find

Close

[TRAVEL IDEAS/ALERTS LINKS]

See Our Top 8 Travel Ideas:

[TICKER]

Houston hotels

New York hotels

Orlando hotels

San Antonio hotels

San Diego hotel reservations

Stockholm hotel rooms

Tampa hotel accommodations

Toronto hotels

[UTILITY BAR]

[LINKS]

Privileges

Travel Ideas

Hotel Deals

[CTA]

Sign in for faster booking or to view your account:

[FIELD]

Username

[FIELD]

Password

[BUTTON]

Sign In

[CHECKBOX]

Remember Me

[LINK]

Forget Username or Password?

[ROLLOVER]

We'll conveniently save your data for the
next time you book.

[CTA]

First time here? Create an account >

[CTA]

Join Privileges for more rewards

[CUSTOMER SERVICE MINI-MODULE]

[HEADER OPTIONS]

Front Desk

Ask Concierge

Need extra help?

[LINK TO CUSTOMER SUPPORT]

Customer Support

[HOTEL DEALS CAROUSEL]

[HIGHLIGHTED DEALS]

[LINK TO HOTEL DEALS PAGE]

Discover more exciting hotel deals >

J

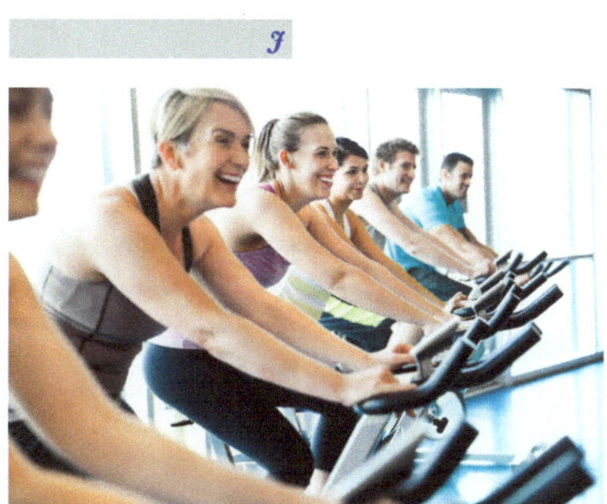

J People exercising on stationary bikes in fitness class. // gym, exercising, health club, healthy lifestyle, spinning class, cycling, sports training, exercise bike, wellbeing, people, indoors, mature women, mature adult, happiness, candid, cardiovascular exercise, togetherness, smiling, adult, leisure activity, lifestyles, young adult, young women, window, 20-24 years, 25-29 years, 30-34 years, 30-39 years, 45-49 years, adults only, alberta, calgary, canada, caucasian ethnicity, color image, exercise equipment, holding, horizontal, image focus technique, looking away, medium group of people, mid adult, mid adult women : 175137743

RESERVATION FORM

[LOGOS]

[NAVS]

[SEARCH MODULE]

[HEADER]

Make a Reservation

[HOTEL ID]

[INTRO COPY]

Now that you've selected the room you want, please confirm the information is correct and reserve.

[CTA]

Already have an account? Sign in now.

[SIGN-IN MODULE]

No profile yet? Skip this step or create an account.

[LINK TO JOIN [illegible] PRIVILEGES AND CREATE PROFILE PAGE]

[CURRENT RESERVATION FORM, WITH AAA OPTION ADDED]

[AGREEMENTS]

Guarantee Policy:

We'll hold your room until 7am the morning following your scheduled arrival date. Kindly let us know if you need to cancel your reservation before then or your credit card will be charged one night's stay plus tax.

[CHECKBOXES]

I have read the guarantee policy and agree to its terms.

Remember my name, address, phone number and email address (not my credit card) for the next time I book. I'm aware my data may be viewed by others who share my computer.

[OPTIONAL VIDEO MODULE]

[HEADER]

[COPY]

Book faster with more rewards!

[BUTTON/LINK TO PRIVILEGES PAGE]

Learn more >

[UPSELL FOR NON-MEMBERS]

[HEADER]

Get maximum rewards with Privileges

[COPY]

Join now to earn points toward your next hotel stay, airline miles and other perks—it takes a minute and is absolutely free!

[CTA CHECKBOXES]

Yes, I'd like to earn points now to apply to my next trip

No, thanks

[BUTTON]

Reserve Now

[FOOTER]

K Businesswoman on the phone at the hotel room. // african ethnicity, hotel, women, one woman only, business travel, business, smiling, hotel suite, telephone, hotel room, people, travel, working, using phone, briefcase, city occupation, one person, only women, text messaging, adult, adults only, beautiful people, beautiful woman, beauty, business finance and industry, businesswoman, busy, capital cities, city life, communication, horizontal, indoors, ljubljana, one young woman only, photography, slovenia, white collar worker, wireless technology, young adults : 527219434

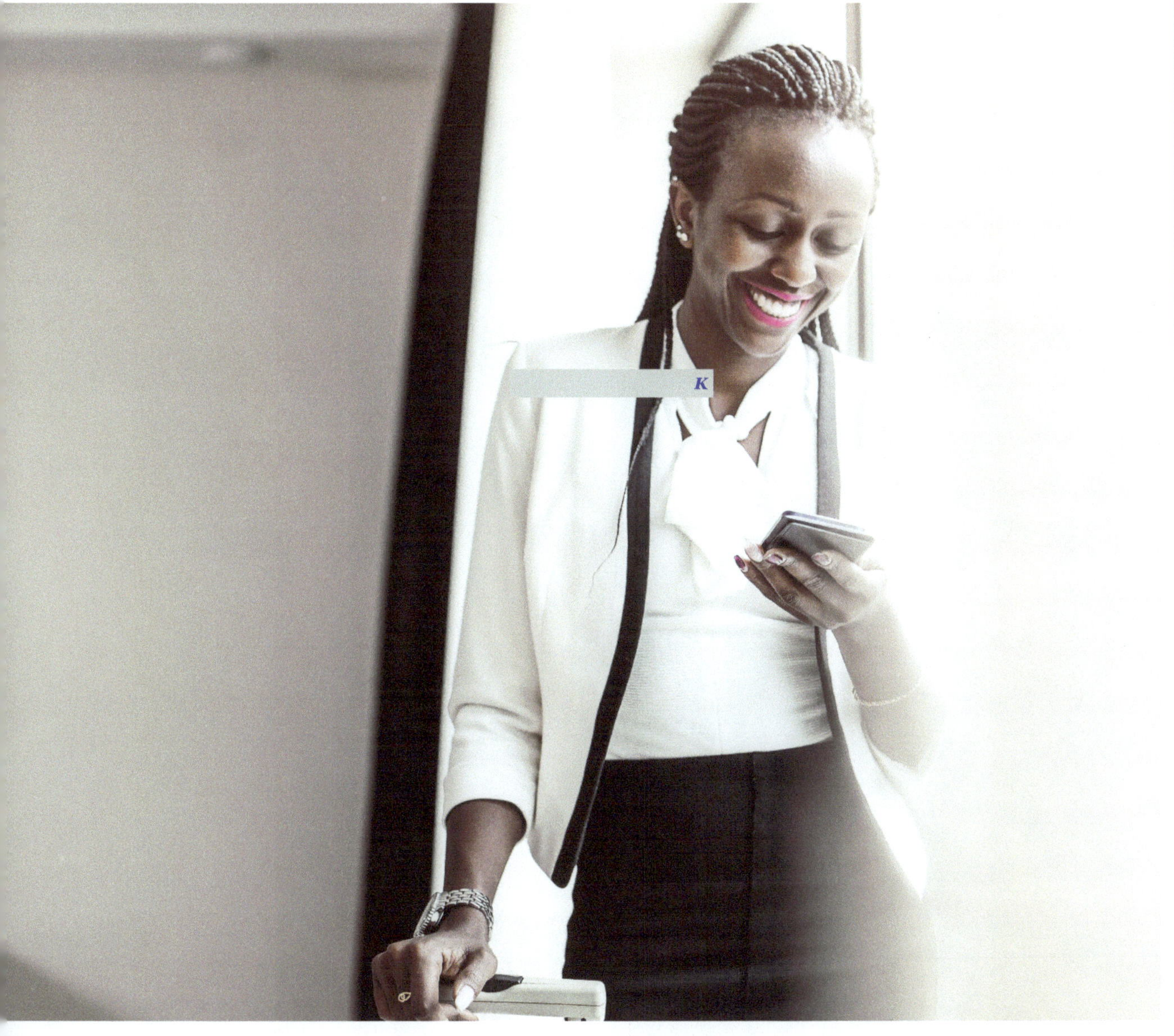

ROOM *for* ERROR

Whoops! You forgot to make a selection. Choose an option now.

Whoops! You forgot to provide some required information. Be sure to fill in all the highlighted fields.

Don't forget to enter your arrival and departure dates.

Don't forget to enter the number of rooms you'll need for your stay.

Don't forget to specify the type of room you'd like to book.

Unfortunately, there are no rooms available on those days. Please specify new dates or select another ********** hotel that fits your trip.

Your search returned too many results, but give it another try with Advanced Search or enter a more specific destination.

Your search returned no results, but give it another try. Consider broadening your search criteria, check for a possible misspelling or get extra help [LINK TO CUSTOMER SUPPORT].

Your search term wasn't recognized, but give it another try. Check for a possible misspelling or get extra help [LINK TO CUSTOMER SUPPORT].

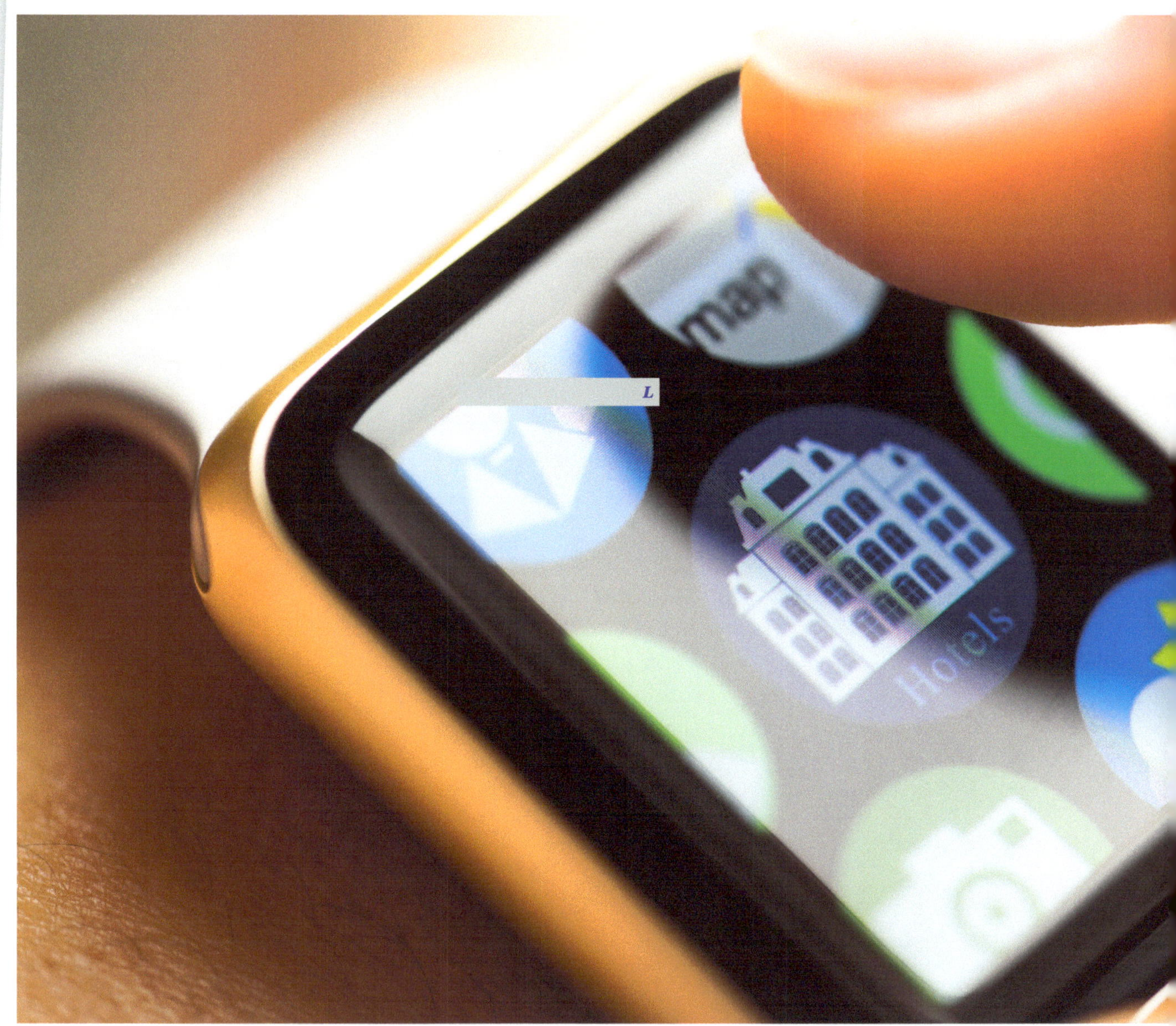
map
L
Hotels

Your [ID/PASSWORD] was not recognized, but double-check your information and try again. Did you forget your username or password [LINK TO CURRENT PAGE/PATH]?

Sorry, that [ID/PASSWORD] is taken. Try another one, or add a familiar word or number to your current selection.

Your [ID/PASSWORD] was not recognized. Double-check your information and try again. If you misplaced your ID, contact your licensing agency for the number. If you're experiencing a system error, please let us know [LINK TO CUSTOMER SUPPORT].

Your special rate ID was not recognized. Please double-check the number and reenter it.

Almost there. But you don't have enough points for a free night yet. Why not buy more points [LINK TO BUY POINTS].

L Finger touching hotel app icon on smart watch screen. // hotel, making a reservation, travel, blue, close-up, color image, connection day, device screen, equipment, finger, hand, holding, horizontal, image focus technique, internet, liquid-crystal display, mobile app, photography, portable information device, smart watch, technology, touch screen, touching, tourism, turkey - middle east, wearable computer, wireless technology, wrist : 665127660

ASSIGNED SEARCH

Constraints:

Yahoo:

Title (40 characters including spaces)

1 Description Line (70 characters including spaces)

Google (same for MSN/AOL/Ask.com when used):

Title (25 characters including spaces)

Description Line 1 (35 characters including spaces)

Description Line 2 (35 characters including spaces)

Yahoo:

Apply for Banking in Seven Minutes
Free checking with no monthly fees.
4.75% APY savings.
Learn more.

What's Better than Free Checking?
Combining it with our high yield 4.75% APY savings.
Learn more.

High or Low Balance?
No monthly checking fees.
Sign up for low-balance alerts.
Learn more.

Google:

Seven Minutes to
All you need for free checking.
4.75% APY savings. Learn more.

Like Our Free Checking?
Try 's exclusive high yield
4.75% APY savings.
Learn more.

High or Low Balance?
No monthly checking fees.
Sign up for low-balance alerts.
Learn more.

MORE WAYS *to* SAY *the* SAME

ATM

Constraints:

Yahoo:

Title (40 characters including spaces)

1 Description Line (70 characters including spaces)

Google (same for MSN/AOL/Ask.com when used):

Title (25 characters including spaces)

Description Line 1 (35 characters including spaces)

Description Line 2 (35 characters including spaces)

Yahoo:

ATM Worth Switching For

Open an account. We don't charge for ATM cash withdrawals. Learn more.

We Never Charge for Getting Cash at ATMs

even gives you cash back on debit card purchases. Learn more.

No ATM Withdrawal Fees at

We don't charge for withdrawals at our 3,720 ATMs. Learn more.

Google:

No Charge for Getting Cash

Open an account. We don't charge for ATM withdrawals. Learn more.

No ATM Withdrawal Fees

even gives you cash back on debit card purchases. Learn more.

Save More with ATM

We don't charge for withdrawals at our 3,720 ATMs. Learn more.

BANKING

Yahoo:

Change is Good—Switch to Banking
Free checking with no monthly fees. 4.75% APY savings.
Learn more.

Checking and Savings—Quite a Pair
Free checking with no monthly fees. 4.75% APY savings.
Learn more.

A Few Ways Makes Banking Easy
Free checks for life, no monthly fee. 4.75% APY savings.
Learn more.

Google:

Switch to Banking
Free checking with no monthly fees.
4.75% APY savings. Learn more.

Makes Banking Fun
Smile. Enjoy free checking.
4.75% APY savings. Learn more.

Win-Win with Banking
Switch to free checking. Enjoy
4.75% APY savings. Learn more.

BENEFITS

Yahoo:

You'll Like the Benefits of Banking
No monthly checking fees. 4.75% APY savings.
Learn more.

More Benefits When You Switch to
Seven minutes to no-fee paperless banking and bill pay.
Learn more.

Likes to Say "No Fees" and "Free"
Free checking with no monthly fees. 4.75% APY savings.
Learn more.

Google:

More Benefits with
Free checks with no monthly fees.
4.75% APY savings. Learn more.

Switch to Benefits
Get paperless banking and bill pay
all in seven minutes. Learn more.

Benefits You'll Like
Enjoy free checks with no monthly
fee. 4.75% APY savings. Learn more.

FREE CHECKING

Yahoo:

Switch to [redacted] Free Checking Online
All you need are seven minutes and a dollar
to get going.
Learn more.

Get Free Checking That's Really Free
No monthly account fees plus free checks for
life at [redacted].
Learn more.

Google:

Get [redacted] Free Checking
All you need are seven minutes and
a dollar to get going.
Learn more.

"Really" Free Checking
No monthly account fees plus free
checks for life at [redacted].
Learn more.

SAVINGS

Yahoo:

It's a Online-Exclusive
Open a high yield savings account and earn 4.75% APY. Learn more.

Savings to Bank On
With 4.75% APY and easy online enrollment why wait? Learn more.

Switch to Savings
Apply online. In seven minutes you could have 4.75% APY. Learn more.

Google:

Savings = 4.75% APY
Why wait to open a high yield savings account? Learn more.

Savings to Bank On

4.75% APY and easy enrollment.

Sign up today. Learn more.

M

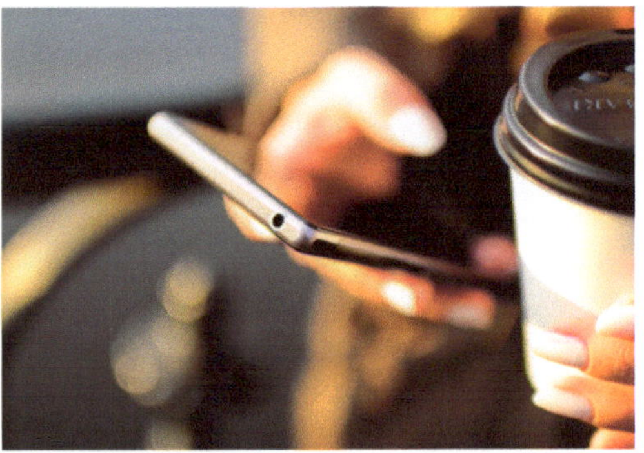

M coffee, contact, email, hands, mobile phone, smartphone, technology, texting, touch, touchscreen, waiting

Switch to 75% Savings
Apply online. In seven minutes you'll have 4.75% APY. Learn more.

N

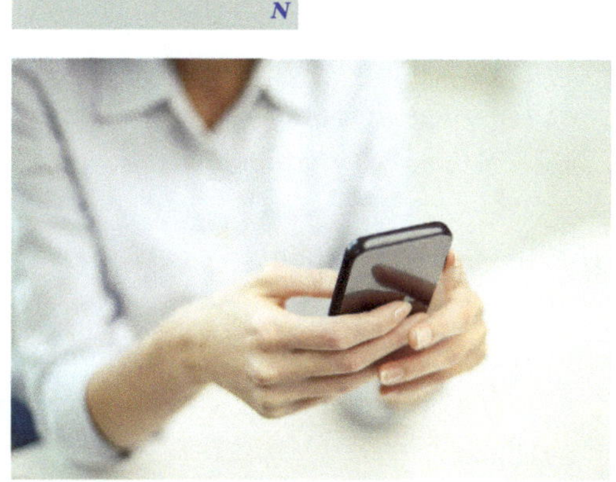

N Close up of woman hands texting message on smartphone at office. // app, application, beautiful, body part, browsing, business, businesswoman, cell, cellphone, chatting, closeup, communicating, communication, concept, connection, conversation, entrepreneur, female, gadget, girl, hands, home, human, indoors, internet, learning, leisure, manager, message, mobile, networking, office, online, people, person, phone, room, sitting, smartphone, sms, social, studying, table, technology, texting, wifi, witless, woman, young : 38674783

AUGMENTED REALITY WHALE

First Draft 'The Evolution of Storytelling'

[BARKER INTRO]

Let's welcome the ~~Leviathan~~ on its maiden voyage. Its crusty barnacles bear out the duration of its journey. Observe the sturdiness of the gondola, harnessed to the ~~Leviathan's~~ stern. The complex weave of saddles and stirrups ensured it made it safely through the storm.

The ~~Leviathan's~~ body itself was grown from the life threads of a whale. There are no less than a hundred species tangled into its design. Countless creatures, fitted together, compose a vast web of life, in ever-shifting balance.

Look—the ~~Leviathan~~ is spewing glowing Baby ~~Huxleys~~! They're making their way toward us now. See how they dart down, attracted to our tablets.

[Terrace area: The ~~Huxleys~~ swim closer.]

Take a closer look. ~~Huxleys~~ are made of the life chains of medusas, jellyfish, and other venomous sea creatures, their bodies are bio-iridescent—an effect heightened by their thick translucent flesh. They gather lightning, and feed the sub-level energy of the ship, delivering electricity to run the human systems.

Full-grown ~~Huxleys~~ are nervous beasts, dangerous in untrained hands, but essential for cloud penetration. They're not just ferocious but practically indestructible; their fishy guts can survive almost any fall. You can pinch them at your own risk.

[ANNOUNCER CLOSE]

World building, powered by hn to ed advances the study of immersive and collaborative storytelling as it intersects with emergent technologies. It's a powerful new narrative process destined to impact the future of entertainment and the richly detailed world becomes a container for countless stories.

How many ways can you tell your story? How many ways will you envision it? Soon you'll be experiencing stories at a level of freedom, scale, and immersion not yet imagined.

New Requirements

Objectives:

- Physically engage visitors with 2 in 1 devices
- Showcase 2 in 1s as best of both worlds: ~~a tablet when you want it, a laptop when you need it~~
- Connect 2 in 1s to the ~~Leviathan~~ experience and **********
- Connect this story directly to visitor's daily aspirations in a natural and intuitive way

Key Phrases:

- ~~Tablet when you want it, laptop when you need it~~
- 2 in 1s offer the best of tablet and laptop experiences
- Full laptop performance with the freedom of a tablet
- Next generation performance enables the next generation of content
- ~~Leviathan~~ is the evolution of entertainment enabled by technology
- 2 in 1s enable next generation interactivity through next generation performance

Experience Outline:

Setup

- Staffer holds a 2 in 1 device in laptop mode: while the device is still in laptop mode.
- Staffer: "Welcome to ~~Leviathan~~: The Evolution of Storytelling. An innovative new 2 in 1 storytelling experience imagined by . We created this experience with the power of a laptop…"
- Staffer takes the 2 in 1 apart, and hands the guest the tablet
- Staffer: "but you can experience it with the freedom of a tablet"

Introduction

- Staffer directs the guest's attention toward the ~~Huxleys~~ in the frame
- Staffer: "The ~~Leviathan~~ is inspired by the steampunk novels of , where scientists create fantastical new creatures, from giant flying whales, to the small and durable airships we see here, called ~~Huxleys~~"

2 in 1: Powerful Play

- Staffer instructs the guest to select one ~~Huxley~~ from the cloud by touching the screen
- The ~~Huxley~~ "tethers" to the guest
- Staffer: "With the power of a 2 in 1 and this new story platform, we can step inside this new world"

2 in 1: Powerful Interaction

- Staffer instructs the guest to interact with their ~~Huxley~~ through the touch screen
  / Poke the ~~Huxley~~ to provoke a "shy kitten" response
  / Swipe to "spin" the ~~Huxley~~ which makes it dizzy
  / Pinch to draw the ~~Huxley~~ closer to you
- Staffer: "The power of a 2 in 1 enables new PERSPECTIVES and new ways to PLAY within rich new story worlds."

2 in 1: Opens powerful new worlds

- Staffer instructs the guest to interact with their ~~Huxley~~ through the movement of the screen
  / Move away from the ~~Huxley~~, and it will follow you… chase it when it retreats
- Staffer instructs the guest to "release" their ~~Huxley~~, and directs the guest's attention to the swarm of digital creatures overhead
- Staffer: "With the power of a 2 in 1, we can create and experience story worlds with a level of freedom, scale and immersion yet unimagined."

Next Steps

- Staff directs visitors to other demo stations
- Staff encourages visitors to come back to the ~~Intel~~ booth for the ~~Leviathan~~ "spotlight" experience @ *X* time.

Final

REF	VISUAL: WHAT IS HAPPENING ON-STAGE OR ON-SCREEN	AUDIO: WHAT IS BEING SAID OR HEARD
1.0	What is happening just prior to demo	SPEAKER: Script "The incredible capability of 3D and Virtual Reality technology will not only change the way we play games in our homes but the way we engage our children and tell stories. We'll no longer be restricted by a flat book with simple pages and pictures…we can open up a world of storytelling never before imagined. Why just imagine a world when you actually see yourself immersed in the story. Now your favorite characters will not just roam around the pages in your book but actually walk and fly around your very own room."
2.0	IMAGE or Visuals on screen	Script "I'm going to share with you for the first time a project we call ~~Leviathan~~. (whale swims across screens in 2D)"

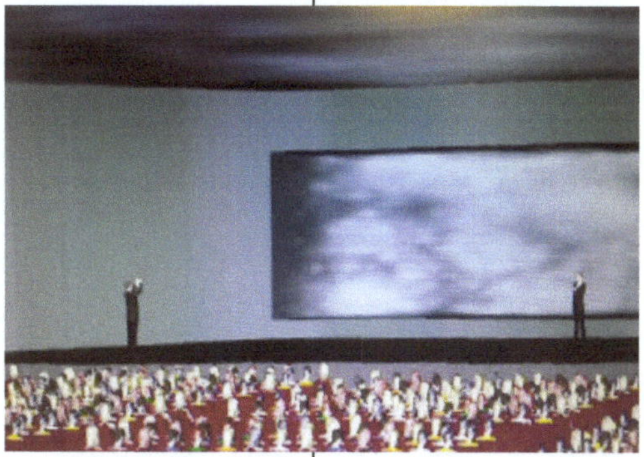

3.0	IMAGE or Visuals on screen 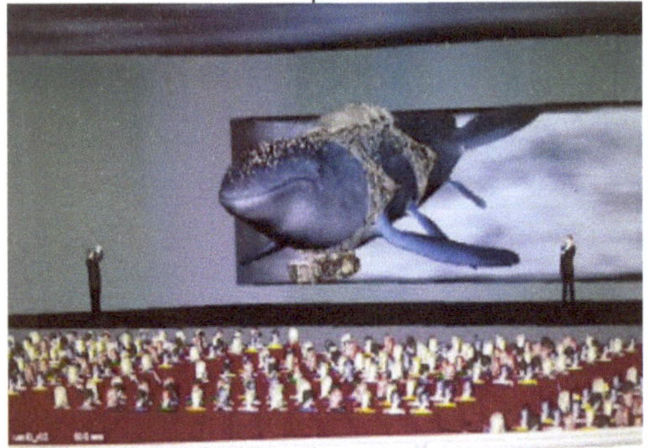	SPEAKER: Script "Sitting with your family and your 2in1 or tablet you can bring the story to life in ways you never thought possible. Today, let's not imagine what a giant whale that swims through the air would look like… let's EXPERIENCE it…the sight, the sound, the motion…all of it. (pause here, sound full, the whale emerges from the screens)"
4.0	IMAGE or Visuals on screen 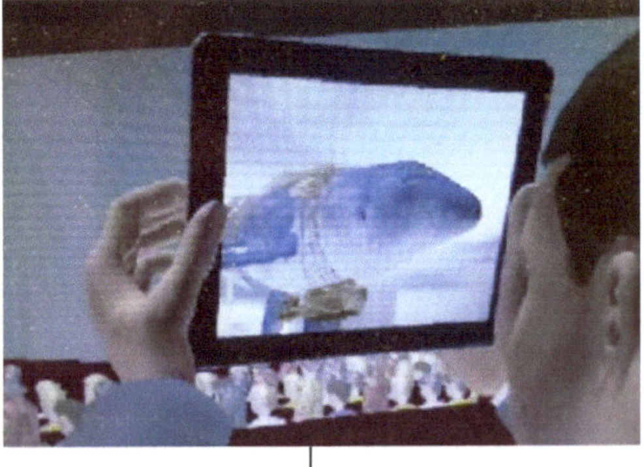	SPEAKER: Script "We have cameras placed throughout room that are there to capture all the action, but notice the person on stage and in the audience. They are able to track and follow our giant friend and see him from multiple angles."

5.0	IMAGE or Visuals on screen	SPEAKER: (Pause here to let the whale swim and go back into the screen) Script "The ~~Leviathan~~ becomes part of your 3D world, swimming in the room with you, creating not just a story, but an immersive, memorable experience that will change the way you look at storytelling forever. (Pause here to let the whale swim and go back into the screen) These are the kinds of experiences we can now create with the amazing performance of ba se ca zi technology."

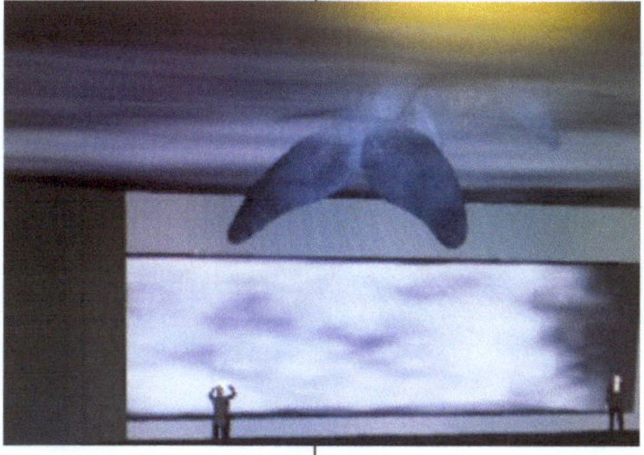

P Augmented reality whale. // Whale rendering by USC World Building Media Lab

FEEDBACK

HI
GUYS

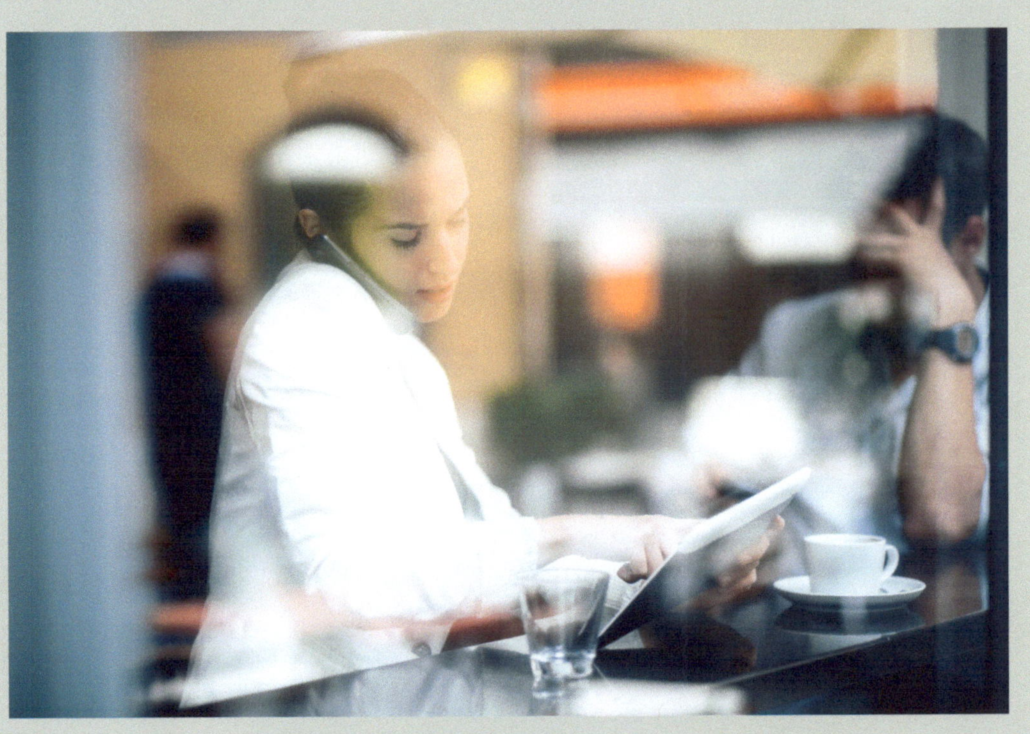

o

I told the Keynote team that we would work on this in the morning, and send back some adaptations - will be a good compression point to make sure we have a single sentence for:

- What is the world of the ~~Leviathan~~

- What is the big deal about digital storytelling

Nothing like a little flame to finish the sauce. ;]

~~Andrew~~

O Busy businesswoman talking on phone and using tablet computer in coffee shop. // authentic, beautiful, break, business, businesswoman, cafe, candid, caucasian, chat, coffee, communication, computer, conversation, corporate, cup, diner, discussion, executive, female, hispanic, internet, job, laptop, latin, lifestyle, man, manger, modern, people, person, portrait, professional, real, reflections, restaurant, smartphone, suit, talk, talking, talking on phone, tea, technology, white, window, woman, work, working, young : 28222558

CAMERA AD REVISIONS

Bruna,

- "Sharp Shooter" is great.
- "Wiggle-detector" is so close. I think there is a better solution for wiggles here than just detection. But, I love that "wiggles" puts one right in mom's mindset.
- In this sample, I miss the personality of Sample 1's Screen 5 rest-state header and fullscreen description.

Thanks,

~~Mike~~

CONTENT MIGRATION: AFFINITY OR ATTRIBUTE?

P `Mother with children playing with sand on beach. //` asian, child, mother, mom, play, kid, beach, asia, mum, parent, day, active, daughter, love, outside, sandcastle, summer, vacation, fun, seaside, woman, healthy, sand, blue, brother, coast, enjoying, female, game, girl, happy, joy, nature, ocean, outdoors, people, person, recreation, relations, sea, seashore, sister, sitting, sky, sunny, three, together, warm, water : 92762122

Q beach, salt water, sand, sea, seawater, steps, summer, vacation, water, waves, public domain images

Bruna, Today, for example, it was explained to me that "Beaches" are an Attribute and "Family" is an Affinity. To me these are both Nouns that describe things, and till date my specific understanding of the word Affinity as we've used it is simply the way to describe some sort of "Thing" concept. A thing (in the context of the new website) is any Thing that is NOT a Member Category, Sub-Category, or Member Attribute. With this understanding, I will defer to [Ca de er a] for the very specific delineation of which specific nouns are being referred to as "Attributes" versus which are being referred to as "Affinities". If I were to guess, I'd assume that [th f if s"] already has a list of "Attributes", and therefore things not on that list would probably now be called "Affinities". Unfortunately, I cannot differentiate between Beaches and Family and thus leave the final decision to [ch cri "Af]. Hope this is helpful.

P

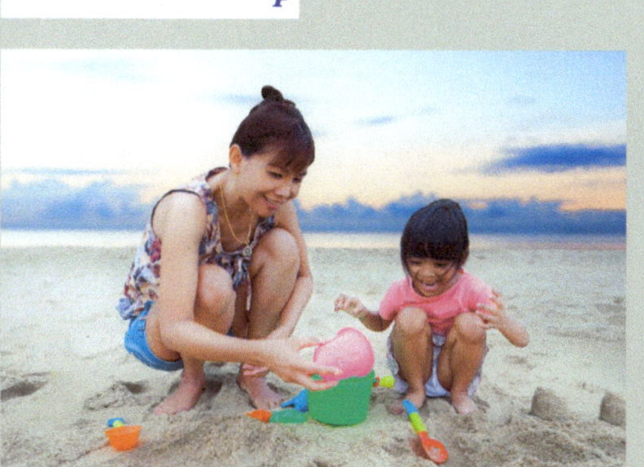

Q

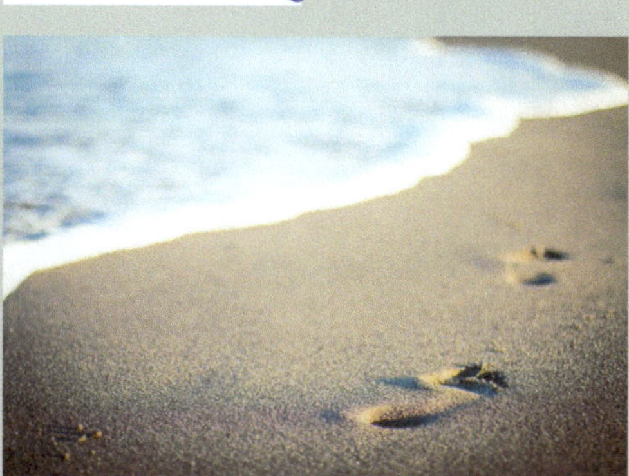

SEARCH ENGINE OPTIMIZER

Bruna,

SEO states more information is needed on the purpose, content and structure of this page in order to make SEO recommendations:

Brochure pages for specific hotel locations require their own unique content. No matter the source, this information should be restructured to reflect original content, incorporating keywords with geo-targeted components.

For example, a hotel in Abilene, Texas should make use of the geo-targeted keywords “Abilene hotels” and “Abilene hotel” as they have the highest search volume. But other related keywords should not be overlooked. The following keywords should be used as support throughout the content and META keywords (though the emphasis should be placed on the “hotel” keywords previously discussed): Abilene lodging, Abilene Texas hotel, Abilene Texas hotels, Abilene Texas lodging, Abilene TX hotel, Abilene TX hotels, Abilene TX lodging.

An H1 header tag on each page should contain both the location and the word “hotel”, so “Hotel in Abilene, TX” would be an acceptable page header.

The Title tag and Meta description must also contain the geo-targeted keyword reflective of the hotel location. This will ensure that the page will harness the power of the geo-targeted specificity in search.

THE CONSULTANT SAID

R Happy business team making high five at office. // achievement, beautiful, bureau, business, businessman, businesswoman, collaboration, colleague, concept, cooperation, corporate, creative, entrepreneurs, gesture, group, happy, high five, hindu, indoors, international, man, many, multiethnic, multiracial, office, partner, partnership, people, person, professional, smiling, startup, success, team, teamwork, together, togetherness, woman, young : 71370912

[COMMENTS FIELD]

Awkward

Awkward

Add back in the authentication paragraph.

More compelling head.

Format: No widow/orphan control.

Be more engaging/experiential.

See Recommended Messaging for the Affluent.

Link to Event Ticket intake form.

Don't list specific merchants as they will not be available.

Assumes the cardholder is reading sequentially.

Revise for [illegible] tone.

Most want lowest fare. Stress convenience over luxury.

Revise.

Revise.

Edit this original copy.

??

Revise.

R

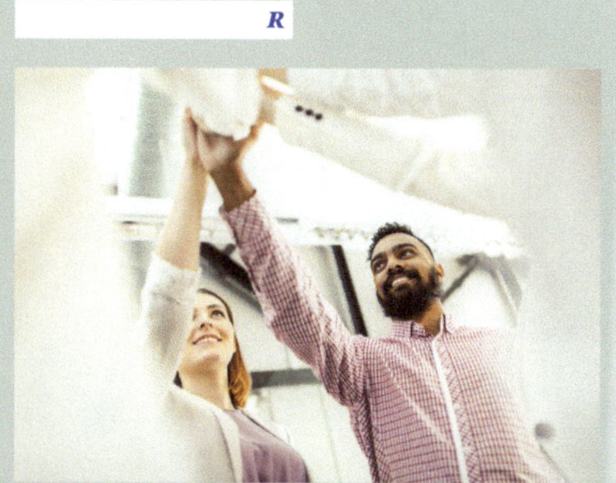

QUICK QUESTION

Bruna, How can we communicate that the option to purchase a preferred parking pass is the only thing that is an exclusive benefit to holders? The viewing area and lounge are included in the ticket price but you don't have to have to buy a ticket, only the parking pass. E.g.: preferred viewing area, VIP lounge, and option to purchase preferred parking pass (just for cardholders).

FORWARDED

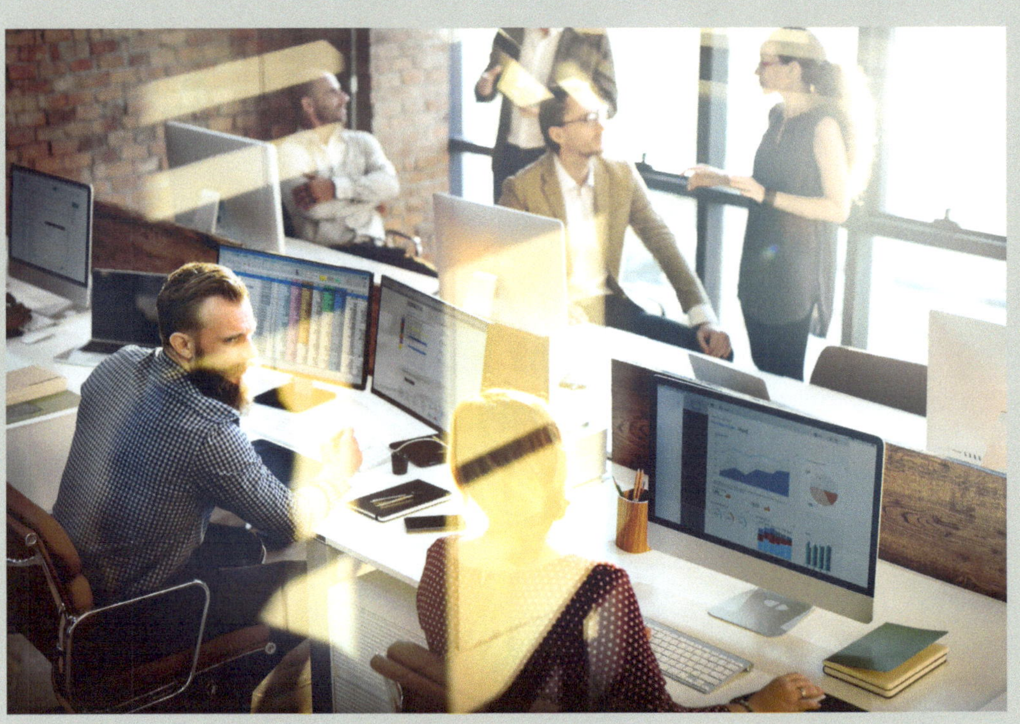

s

From: ~~T~~
Date: Fri, 15 Feb 2008 09:18:00 -0800
To: ~~Michael~~
Cc: Bruna Mori
Conversation: Help?
Subject: Re: Help?

Hi ~~Michael~~! I am actually out of the office on PTO today, but I think Bruna would have time to help you out. She's a good brainstormer. You can reach her today at x5444. I've also copied her here.

~~T~~

On 2/15/08 6:57 AM, ~~Michael~~ wrote:

Hey - I'm in need of some copy brainstorming around one very small but important and vexing problem. Do you and/or one of your brilliant copywriters have a few minutes to talk something through with me?

S Business Team Discussion Meeting Corporate Concept. // business, marketing, team, corporate, office, people, sales, working, accounting, adult, african, asian, brainstorming, businessmen, businesswomen, busy, casual, cheerful, collaboration, communication, computer, contemporary, cooperation, coworker, dashboard, descent, discussion, diverse, diversity, employee, ethnicity, financial, folder, group, interaction, messy, multiethnic, organization, planning, smiling, stationery, support, talking, teamwork, technology, togetherness, worker, young : 393605650

BILL
CODE

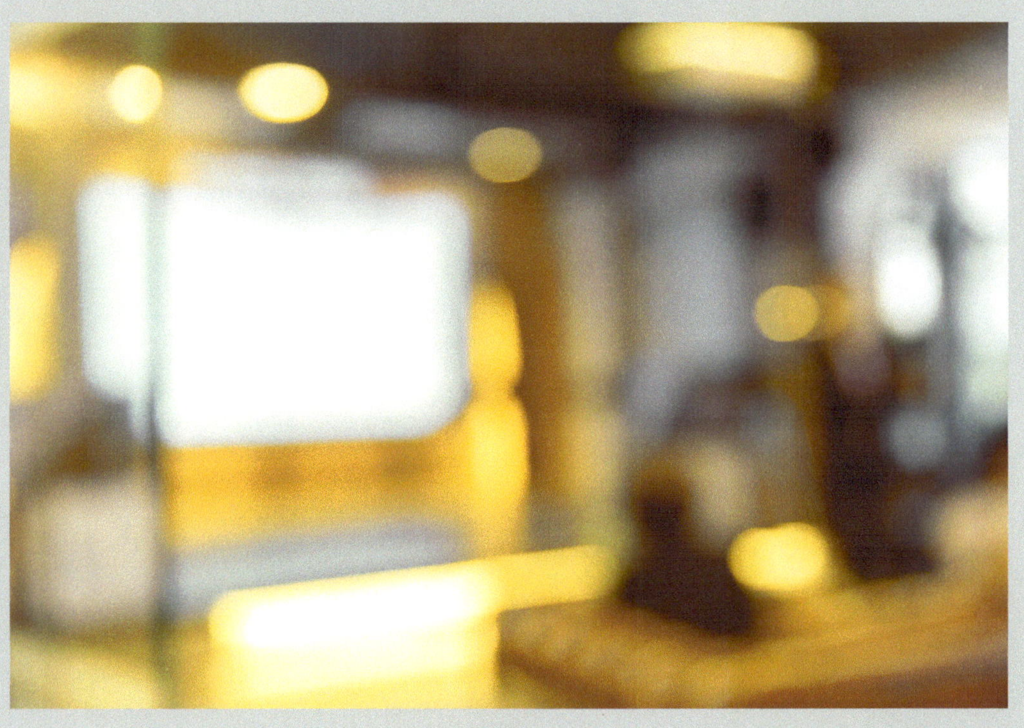

T

Hello! Event projects are, until further notice, always billed to 12906, so that's an easy one. Incentives is 15149. We are budget constrained on the latter, so any training time (such as today's call) should be billed to non-bill 15149 instead of labor 15149. ~~Craig~~ can help you with this if that doesn't already make sense.

T abstract background bokeh in meeting business interior office with people blurred, shallow depth of focus. // abstract, background, blurred, blurry, bokeh, bright, bulb, business, businessman, circle, circular, classroom, colleagues, corporate, defocused, education, effect, employees, executive, focus, glitter, glow, glowing, group, hall, illuminated, illumination, indoor, inside, interior, job, light, lightbulb, lobby, manager, meeting, office, people, person, professional, room, shine, sitting, spot, student, talking, training, twinkling, young : 573739870

DEAR ASSOCIATES

An e-mail went out a few weeks ago about professional dress at . The intent of the message is not to create a stuffy or uptight environment. Rather, maintain a high level of professionalism in all areas. I'd like to see us elevate our level of professionalism as we are moving to a very professional and nice office environment. Associates should present themselves in a professional manner and be mindful of their presentation as well. I am certain we will have more professional meetings with board members, customers and the public at our new space and we want to be sure to make a professional impression with appearance and dress that is professional.

Monday through Thursday

MEN

Collared button-up long-sleeved dress shirt

Dress slacks

Socks & shoes

Tommy Bahama type shirts with conservative or no print

WOMEN

Dress slacks or skirts

Dresses

Friday-casual day

Dark wash denim with no holes or fray is allowed

Capris - not too casual

Nice T-shirts

Golf Shirts

The NO list:

Flip flops

Shorts

Skorts

Halter tops

Spaghetti straps

Backless tops

T-Shirts

Tank tops

Capris-M-Th

Facial Jewelry or piercings

Leggings/spandex/form fitting clothing

Athletic Shoes/sneakers/Crocs

Revealing or suggestive items

Wrinkled clothing

Sandals for men

Visible tattoos (see HR if you have a visible tattoo)

DISCLAIMER

[ABOVE FOLD]

NO PURCHASE OR OBLIGATION NECESSARY TO ENTER OR WIN. For details on nonpurchase entries see Official Rules [ANCHORS TO OFFICIAL RULES].

[BELOW FOLD]

Official Rules ("Official Rules")

NO PURCHASE OR OBLIGATION NECESSARY TO ENTER OR CLAIM A PRIZE. Non-Purchase Entries and Purchase Entries have an Equal Chance of Winning.

1. Eligibility: Sweepstakes is open to all legal residents of the fifty (50) United States and the District of Columbia, eighteen (18) years of age and older as of 2/1/~~00~~. Commercial card eligibility subject to employer policies regarding sweepstakes. Employees of the ~~International Olympic Committee ("IOC"), U.S. Olympic Committee ("USOC")~~ and each of their respective subsidiaries, affiliates, shareholders, officers, directors, agents, representatives, and employees of ~~U.S.A. Inc.~~, its successors and assigns, ~~International Service Association~~, its successors and assigns and their respective Member financial institutions, and their respective parent companies, subsidiaries, affiliates, prize suppliers, and advertising and promotion agencies of ~~U.S.A. Inc.~~, and each of their respective agents, representatives, officers, directors, shareholders, and employees (all of the above collectively "Releasees"), and each of their immediate family members (spouse, and parents, children, and siblings, and their respective spouses, regardless of where they live) and individuals living in the same households of each of these individuals, whether related or not, of the above are not eligible. Void where prohibited or restricted by law. The Sweepstakes is subject to all applicable federal, state, and local laws and regulations.

2. To Enter: Sweepstakes begins at 12:00:01 a.m. Pacific Time ("PT") on 2/1/~~00~~ and ends at 11:59:59 p.m. PT on 4/30/~~00~~ ("Promotional Period"). Enter one of [3] ways: (1) Automatic Entry: An eligible ® card-holder automatically receives one (1) Sweepstakes entry for each eligible purchase and one (1) bonus Sweepstakes entry for each payment he/she makes of a regular or ongoing bill with his/her card by its required due date during the Promotional Period. Eligible regular and ongoing bill payments are one-time and recurring payments that occur and are paid at least monthly. Such payments may be made online, via U.S. mail, by telephone, or in person. Certain restrictions may apply. Purchases of goods must be at a participating merchant location in the United States. Only eligible purchases or payments made with a card that is not in default under the customer agreement for that account and issued by a participating financial institution in the U.S., and processed through ~~U.S.A. Inc.'s~~ transaction-processing system during the Promotional Period, are eligible for automatic entry. In the event of a dispute as to who submitted a particular cardholder entry, such entry will be deemed to be submitted by the primary person in whose name the card used to enter the Sweepstakes was issued. Account adjustment transactions/returns, cash advances, balance transfers, non-U.S.-dollar purchases, ~~Interlink®~~-processed transactions, purchases authorized by entering a PIN (personal identification number), payment of late fees or over-limit fees, and health and benefit cards are excluded from automatic entry. cards or card numbers that are stolen, fraudulent, tampered with, or otherwise altered are not eligible for

automatic entry. (2) By Online Entry: Only one (1) entry per person/email address/phone number allowed per day for the entire Promotional Period. Entries must be received by 11:59:59 p.m. PT of each day. (3) By Mail: To enter without purchase or obligation and receive 2 entries: Mail a 3″x5″ card hand-printed with complete name, address and day and evening tel. #s, and the words "fi e an ~~2000 Olympic Games Sweepstakes~~" to: ~~2000 Olympic Games Sweepstakes~~, Box 4054, Grand Rapids, MN 55730-4054. Entries must be postmarked by 4/30/~~00~~, and received by 5/7/~~00~~. Enter as often as you wish; only one entry per stamped envelope will be accepted. No mechanical reproductions permitted. Entries become the property of - Me e ~~U.S.A. Inc.~~ and will not be returned.

3. Drawing: On or about 5/15/~~00~~, a random drawing will be conducted under the direction of the Administrator whose decisions are final and binding in all matters relating to the Sweepstakes. Only one prize per person or household.

4. Estimated Odds of Winning: The Grand Prize: 1:6,912,511,345; First Prize: 1:691,251,135; actual odds of winning any prize depends upon the total number of eligible entries received.

5. Prizes: One (1) Grand Prize: A trip for (2) people to the ~~2000~~ Olympic Games ~~in Beijing, China~~, including R/T air (coach) from a major int'l airport nearest winner's home, hotel accommodations for (7) days/(6) nights (8/11/~~00~~-8/17/~~00~~), all ground transportation in ~~Beijing~~ to/ from airport and to scheduled events; two (2) tickets to one event (event is at discretion of Sponsor) per day (excluding arrival and departure

days), two (2) tickets to one (1) guided tour from a selected list of tours (determined by Sponsor), all scheduled meals, and Ti e an at ~~U.S. Olympic Team~~ apparel, and for the winner a $500 Me e up s Gift card & $6,860 in cash that may be used towards the payment of taxes. Approx. Retail Value ("ARV") $22,313; however, value may vary depending upon residence of winner. Any difference in ARV and actual value will not be awarded. Ten (10) First Prizes: A ~~Red Ray™~~ Theater, featuring a 58" 1080p Plasma HDTV, a $500 ********** Gift card, plus $2,885 cash that may be used towards the payment of taxes. ARV $8,885 ea.

Prize Restrictions: The winner and his/her guest must travel on the same itinerary between 8/10/~~00~~ and 8/17/~~00~~. Travel arrangements must be made through Sponsor's agent, on a carrier of Sponsor's choice. Winner and guest are responsible for obtaining all travel documents and travel insurance (and all other forms of insurance) they may wish to obtain (at their own expense) and hereby acknowledge that the Sponsor has not and will not obtain or provide travel insurance or any other form of insurance. In the event that the ~~2000~~ Olympic Games are canceled, the balance of the prize will be awarded in full satisfaction of the prize award. Seat locations for all events will be determined by Sponsor, who also reserves the right to remove or to deny entry to any winner and/or his/her guest who engages in a non-sportsmanlike or disruptive manner, or with the intent to annoy, abuse, threaten, or harass any other person at the game. All event tickets and i e Gift cards are subject to certain terms and conditions as specified by the ~~IOC & USOC~~ and issuer thereon. No substitution, cash equivalent, or transfer of prize permitted except at the sole discretion of the Sponsor. Winner is responsible for all taxes and any other expenses not specifically described above. Winner and guest are responsible for consulting their personal physician regarding any vaccinations or other inoculations that may be required, and obtaining such. The prizes are awarded "AS IS" and WITHOUT WARRANTY OF ANY KIND, express or implied, by Sponsor.

6. Notification: Potential Grand Prize winner will be notified on or about 5/17/~~00~~ via telephone starting at 12:00 p.m. (noon) Central Time ("CT"). If the potential Grand Prize winner does not answer the phone, no message will be left, he/she will be disqualified and, at Sponsor's discretion and time permitting, an alternate winner may be selected and notified. This process will continue, time permitting, until a Grand Prize winner has been determined and verified. First Prize winners notified by mail on or about 5/20/~~00~~. Forfeiture of prize and selection of an alternate winner will result from any of the following: [1] failure of a potential winner to execute and return an Affidavit of Eligibility/ Liability Release, and where legal, a Publicity Release, and a completed IRS Form W-9, within 7-days after notification of such; [2] the return of any notification or prize as undeliverable and [3] any other noncompliance with these Official Rules. If the prize is won by an eligible individual who is not of the legal age of majority in the state of residence ("minor"), the required documents must be confirmed and signed by winner's parent or legal guardian. Winner's travel companion must be of the legal age of majority in his/her state of residence (and at least 18 years of age or older), unless they are an

immediate family member, and must sign a liability release. If a minor, such release must be signed by the parent or legal guardian. By entering the Sweepstakes, entrants, or, if minors, their parent or legal guardian, agree to the use by Sponsor or its designees of their names and photographs/likenesses for advertising and promotional purposes for this and similar promotions, worldwide, and in perpetuity, in any and all forms of media, now known or hereafter devised without compensation except where prohibited by law. Upon request, winner agrees to consent to such in writing.

7. Limitation of Liability: By entering Sweepstakes, entrants, or, if minors, their parents or legal guardians, agree to release, indemnify, and hold harmless the Releasees against any injuries/ losses/ damages/claims/actions and any liability of any kind resulting, in whole or in part, directly or indirectly, from participation in the Sweepstakes or acceptance/possession/use/misuse or nonuse of the prizes awarded. Sweepstakes and Official Rules shall be interpreted in accordance with the laws of the State of California without regard to its principles of conflicts of law. Jurisdiction and venue shall be solely within the State of California. Releasees are not responsible for technical, computer, mechanical, printing, typographical, human or other errors relating to or in connection with the Sweepstakes, including, without limitation, errors which may occur in connection with the administration of the Sweepstakes, the processing of entries or in any Sweepstakes-related material, the announcement of the prizes; or for stolen, lost, late, misdirected, damaged, incomplete, inaccurate, undelivered, delayed

or illegible entries, or postage-due entries or mail; or for electronic, computer, or telephonic malfunction or error, entries which fail to enter into the processing system, or are processed, reported, or transmitted late or incorrectly, or are lost for any reason including computer, telephone, or paper transfer or human or other error. If in the Sponsor's opinion, there is any suspected or actual evidence of electronic or non-electronic tampering with any portion of the Sweepstakes, or if computer viruses, bugs, unauthorized intervention, fraud, or technical difficulties or failures compromise, corrupt, or affect the administration, integrity, security, fairness, or proper conduct of the Sweepstakes, the Sponsor in its sole discretion reserves the right to disqualify any individual who tampers with the entry process and/or void any entries submitted fraudulently, to modify or suspend the Sweepstakes, or to terminate the Sweepstakes and conduct a random drawing and award the prizes using all eligible non-suspect entries received as of the termination date. As a condition of entering the Sweepstakes, entrant or, if a minor, his/her parent or legal guardian, agrees that a) under no circumstances will entrant be permitted to obtain awards for, and entrant hereby waives all rights to claim, punitive, incidental, consequential, or any other damages, other than for actual out-of-pocket expenses, b) all causes of action arising out of or connected with this Sweepstakes or the prize awarded, shall be resolved individually, without resort to any form of class action, and c) any and all claims, judgments, and awards shall be limited to actual out-of-pocket costs incurred and in no event shall entrant be entitled to receive attorneys' fees or other legal costs. Sponsor reserves the right to modify prize award procedures. Any attempt by an entrant or any other individual to deliberately damage any Web site or undermine the legitimate operation of the promotion is a violation of criminal and civil laws and should such an attempt be made, the Sponsor reserves the right to seek damages and other remedies from any such person to the fullest extent permitted by law.

8. Who Won?: For names of winners available after 5/31/~~00~~, mail a SASE to: ~~2000 Olympic Games Winners~~, Box 707, Sayreville, NJ, 08871-0707. Requests must be received no later than 5/15/~~00~~. Requests will be fulfilled when the drawing has been conducted and the winners have been verified.

CONSUMER DISCLOSURE: NO PURCHASE OR OBLIGATION NECESSARY TO ENTER OR WIN. A PURCHASE WILL NOT INCREASE YOUR CHANCES OF WINNING.

CONTRIBUTORS

Bruna Mori is a writer and educator, preoccupied with spatial discourses such as drift of the commodity. Her books of poetry include *BEIGE* (UpsetPress, 2018) and *Dérive* (Meritage Press, 2006). She has published numerous articles and essays, and also taught poetics at the University of California, San Diego, California Institute of the Arts, Southern California Institute of Architecture, and Art Center College of Design. Her MFA and BA degrees were completed at Bard College and the University of California, San Diego. She wrote copy on behalf of agencies and corporations for over a decade.

Kylie King is a designer and architectural theorist living in Providence, Rhode Island. Her work lies at the intersection of Architectural Design, Spatial Politics, and Post-Human Critical Theory. Kylie has presented her work at the HKW in Berlin, is a contributor to *The Expanded Environment* and recently completed a Masters degree in Adaptive Reuse from the Rhode Island School of Design.

Wendy Belt is a designer and creative director based in San Diego, California. She is a graduate of Art Center College of Design. Her design practice specializes in book design and branding in the non-profit, social impact for-profit and artistic spaces. Past publications include artist books for Robert Irwin, Kelsey Brookes and Gisela Colon.

www.ingramcontent.com/pod-product-compliance
Lightning Source LLC
LaVergne TN
LVHW070226110826
845147LV00003B/654
* 9 7 8 1 9 4 7 3 2 2 9 4 3 *